This book belongs to:

....
....
....

Copyright © 2019 by Jumaye Publishing
All rights reserved. This book or any
 portion thereof may not be
reproduced or used in
 any manner
whatsoever without the express
written permission of the publisher
except for the use of brief quotations
in a book review.

Printed by Kindle Direct Publishing

CHECKLIST

....

CHECKLIST

....

- [ ]
- [ ]
- [ ]
- [ ]
- [ ]
- [ ]
- [ ]
- [ ]
- [ ]
- [ ]
- [ ]
- [ ]
- [ ]
- [ ]
- [ ]
- [ ]

STAR METHOD

The **STAR** method is a structured manner of responding to a Interview question by discussing the specific **s**ituation, **t**ask, **A**ction & **r**esult of the situation you are describing.

Situation: That you were in or the task that you needed to accomplish. Describe a specific event not a generalized description of what you have done in the past. Be sure to give enough detail for the interviewer to understand.

Task: What goal were you working towards achieving

Action: Describe the steps you took to address the situation with an appropriate amount of
detail and keep the focus on You Not the team. Use **"I,"** not **"we"** when describing actions.

Result: Describe the outcome of your actions and don't be shy about taking credit for yours. Make sure your answer contains multiple positive results.

Prepare short descriptions of each situation

NOTES

NOTES

Prepare short descriptions of each situation

NOTES

NOTES

Prepare short descriptions of each situation

NOTES

NOTES

Prepare short descriptions of each situation

NOTES

NOTES

Prepare short descriptions of each situation

NOTES

NOTES

Prepare short descriptions of each situation

NOTES

NOTES

Prepare short descriptions of each situation

NOTES

NOTES

Prepare short descriptions of each situation

NOTES

NOTES

Prepare short descriptions of each situation

NOTES

NOTES

Prepare short descriptions of each situation

NOTES

NOTES

Prepare short descriptions of each situation

NOTES

NOTES

Prepare short descriptions of each situation

NOTES

NOTES

Prepare short descriptions of each situation

NOTES

NOTES

Prepare short descriptions of each situation

NOTES

NOTES

Prepare short descriptions of each situation

NOTES

NOTES

Prepare short descriptions of each situation

NOTES

NOTES

Prepare short descriptions of each situation

NOTES

NOTES

Prepare short descriptions of each situation

NOTES

NOTES

Prepare short descriptions of each situation

NOTES

NOTES

Prepare short descriptions of each situation

NOTES

NOTES

Prepare short descriptions of each situation

NOTES

NOTES

Prepare short descriptions of each situation

NOTES

NOTES

Prepare short descriptions of each situation

NOTES

NOTES

Prepare short descriptions of each situation

NOTES

NOTES

Prepare short descriptions of each situation

NOTES

NOTES

Prepare short descriptions of each situation

NOTES

NOTES

Prepare short descriptions of each situation

NOTES

NOTES

Prepare short descriptions of each situation

NOTES

NOTES

Prepare short descriptions of each situation

NOTES

NOTES

Prepare short descriptions of each situation

NOTES

NOTES

Prepare short descriptions of each situation

NOTES

NOTES

Prepare short descriptions of each situation

NOTES

NOTES

Made in the USA
Coppell, TX
13 May 2025

49277844R00056